AMAZING SNAKES!

BALL PYTHONS

BY DAVY SWEAZEY

EPIC

BELLWETHER MEDIA • MINNEAPOLIS, MN

EPIC BOOKS are no ordinary books. They burst with intense action, high-speed heroics, and shadows of the unknown. Are you ready for an Epic adventure?

This edition first published in 2014 by Bellwether Media, Inc.

No part of this publication may be reproduced in whole or in part without written permission of the publisher. For information regarding permission, write to Bellwether Media, Inc., Attention: Permissions Department, 5357 Penn Avenue South, Minneapolis, MN 55419.

Library of Congress Cataloging-in-Publication Data

Sweazey, Davy.
  Ball Pythons / by Davy Sweazey.
     pages cm. – (Epic: Amazing Snakes!)
  Summary: "Engaging images accompany information about ball pythons. The combination of high-interest subject matter and light text is intended for students in grades 2 through 7"– Provided by publisher.
  Audience: Ages 7-12.
  Includes bibliographical references and index.
  ISBN 978-1-62617-088-9 (hbk. : alk. paper)
  1. Ball python–Juvenile literature. I. Title.
  QL666.O63.S94 2014
  597.96'78–dc23
                              2013034882

TABLE OF CONTENTS

WHAT ARE BALL PYTHONS?

Ball pythons are thick snakes with narrow necks and triangle-shaped heads. They grow up to 6 feet (1.8 meters) long.

4

WHERE BALL PYTHONS LIVE

ball python range =

Ball pythons live in **tropical** forests and savannahs in Africa. They usually stay on the ground and slither through grass. They use belly scales called scutes to move forward.

Straight to the Point

Many snakes slither back and forth. Ball pythons slither straight ahead like caterpillars.

Ball pythons hide during the day. Brown and tan patches **camouflage** their bodies. They sometimes rest in empty animal **burrows**. At night, they come out to eat.

AMBUSHING PREY

Ball pythons usually hunt for small **rodents**. They use their **pits** and forked tongue to find **prey**. Then they **ambush** the prey with a quick bite.

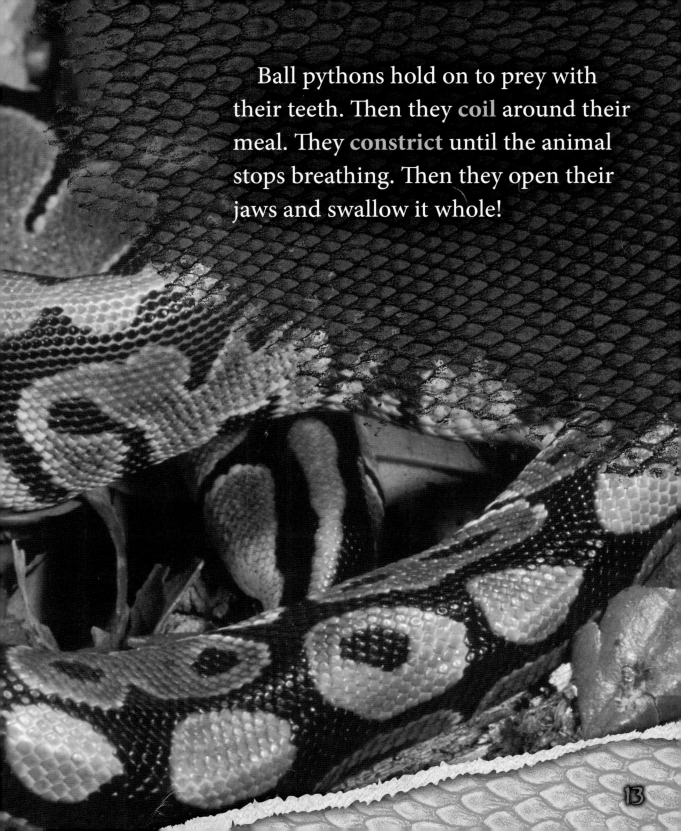

Ball pythons hold on to prey with their teeth. Then they **coil** around their meal. They **constrict** until the animal stops breathing. Then they open their jaws and swallow it whole!

Ball pythons are not safe from **predators.**
Large birds and other **reptiles** sometimes
attack them. Cobras will sink their fangs

COILING FROM PREDATORS

A ball python usually does not bite in **defense**. Instead, it curls into a ball and hides its head inside. This behavior earned the ball python its name.

Fit for a King
In Europe, ball pythons are called royal pythons. According to legend, ancient royalty in Africa would wear ball pythons as jewelry.

Female ball pythons lay eggs. A female coils around her eggs to protect them. She stays with them and does not eat until the eggs hatch. She might have to wait for three months!

Make a Break
A baby ball python has a special tooth on its nose. The tooth helps the snake break out of its egg.

SPECIES PROFILE

SCIENTIFIC NAME:	*PYTHON REGIUS*
NICKNAME:	ROYAL PYTHON
AVERAGE SIZE:	3-6 FEET (1-1.8 METERS)
HABITATS:	TROPICAL FORESTS, SAVANNAHS
COUNTRIES:	BENIN, BURKINA FASO, CAMEROON, CENTRAL AFRICAN REPUBLIC, CHAD, DEMOCRATIC REPUBLIC OF THE CONGO, GAMBIA, GHANA, GUINEA, GUINEA-BISSAU, IVORY COAST, LIBERIA, MALI, NIGER, NIGERIA, REPUBLIC OF CONGO, SENEGAL, SIERRA LEONE, SOUTH SUDAN, TOGO, UGANDA
VENOMOUS:	NO
HUNTING METHOD:	AMBUSH AND CONSTRICTION
COMMON PREY:	RATS, MICE

GLOSSARY

ambush—to attack by surprise

burrows—homes dug in the ground by animals

camouflage—to hide an animal or thing by helping it blend in with the surroundings

coil—to wrap around

constrict—to squeeze until breathing stops

defense—protection

fangs—sharp, hollow teeth; cobras use fangs to attack.

pits—heat-sensing holes around the mouth; ball pythons use pits to hunt at night.

predators—animals that hunt other animals for food

prey—animals that are hunted by other animals for food

reptiles—cold-blooded animals that have scales or hard layers covering their bodies

rodents—small animals that usually gnaw on their food

savannahs—flat, grassy land without many trees

scales—small plates of skin that cover and protect a snake's body

scutes—large, rough scales on the stomach of a snake

22 **tropical**—part of a hot, rainy region near the equator

TO LEARN MORE

At the Library

McCarthy, Colin. *Reptile*. New York, N.Y.: DK Pub., 2012.

Sexton, Colleen. *Pythons*. Minneapolis, Minn: Bellwether Media, 2010.

Time For Kids: Snakes! New York, N.Y.: HarperCollins Publishers, 2005.

On the Web

Learning more about ball pythons is as easy as 1, 2, 3.

1. Go to www.factsurfer.com.

2. Enter "ball pythons" into the search box.

3. Click the "Surf" button and you will see a list of related Web sites.

With factsurfer.com, finding more information is just a click away.

INDEX